To
my husband, Rex,
my children, Rex, Jr. and Sue
and to Dad

Beginning-to-Read
Riddles and Jokes

Alice Thompson Gilbreath
illustrated by Susan Perl

Follett Publishing Company

Chicago

Library of Congress Catalog Card Number: 67-21164

ISBN 0-695-47740-4

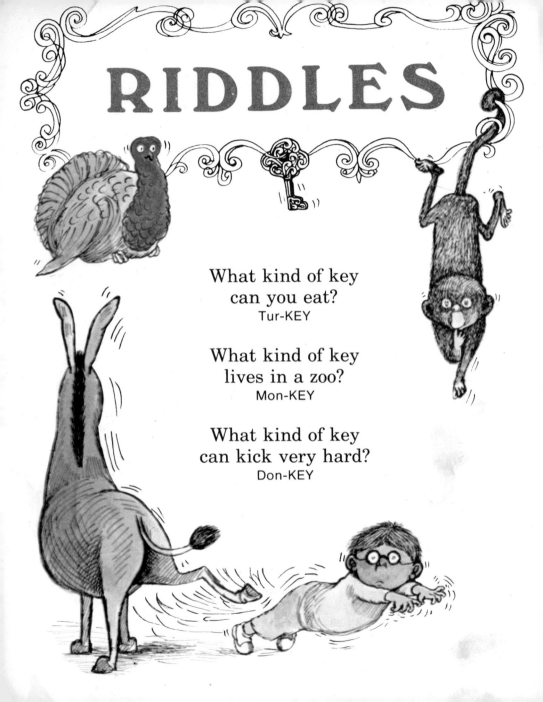

RIDDLES

What kind of key
can you eat?
Tur-KEY

What kind of key
lives in a zoo?
Mon-KEY

What kind of key
can kick very hard?
Don-KEY

How long is a shoe?
1 foot long

What did the glove say to the hand?
"I've got you covered."

How did a belt break the law?
It held up some pants.

What can you make
that you can't see?
Noise

When is your mouth like the sky?
When a tooth comes out,
because there's SPACE

What day of the week is best for boys?
Sunday (SON-day)

What day of the week is lazy?
SAT-urday

What day of the week is a good cook?
Friday (FRY-day)

How do you know the elephant will stay
for a long time when he comes to visit?
He brings his trunk.

On which side does a bear have thick fur?
On the outside

What flying animal is always
found at a baseball game?
Bat

When a Cub Scout jumps into a lake,
what is the first thing he does?
Gets wet

When were you twins?
When you were two

You are my brother but I am not
your brother. Who am I?
Your sister

What letter is a bird?
J (Jay)

What letter can sting?
B (Bee)

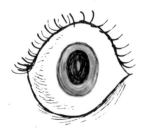

What letter is part of the face?
I (Eye)

What letter does not need glasses?
C (See)

10

Which animal
did not tell the truth?
Lion (lyin')

Which dog always knows what time it is?
Watch dog

Why did the little pig eat so much?
He was making a hog of himself.

What is a kitten after it is four days old?
Five days old

What number is not hungry?
8 (Ate)

What color is noisy?
YELL-ow

Which year can jump very high?
Leap year

How do we know the ocean is friendly?
It waves.

In what way are a bed, a lion,
and a river alike?
Each has springs.

Why did the big rope scold the little rope?
It was knotty (naughty).

What kind of snake is most like a penny?
COPPER-head

What fruit is on a nickel?
Date

Which coin does a skunk have?
Cent (scent)

Why does the mailman have a blue truck?
To carry the mail

What song did the frying pan sing?
"Home on the Range"

JOKES

Horse: "Your feet make me think of my dad."
Dog: "That's silly. Why would my feet
make you think of your dad?"
Horse: "They're paws (pa's)."

Girl: "Are you going to take the bus home?"
Boy: "No. My mother would only make me
take it back."

Sue: "What was the hardest thing about
learning to roller skate?"
Ted: "The floor."

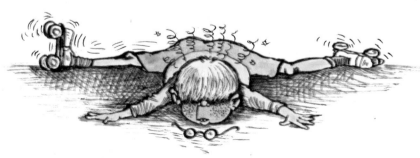

Jack: "Ron's mother won't let him keep frogs at their house, so he found some water and put them in."

Mother: "Oh, that's fine. Where did he find the water?"

Jack: "In our bathtub."

Jill: "I have a dog."
Sam: "A bird dog?"
Jill: "No."
Sam: "A poodle?"
Jill: "No."
Sam: "What kind?"
Jill: "A hot dog!"

John: "What would you say if you saw
a ghost?"
Sue: "Not a word. I'd just run!"

Little Ghost: "I'm going to sing with the
big ghosts today."
Very Little Ghost: "What are you going to sing?"
Little Ghost: "A-Haunting We Will Go."

Tim: "I don't like Sally. I don't want
            to go to her birthday party."

Mother: "You must go, Tim. Now, what would
            you like to give her?"

Tim: "Measles."

Bill: "I hit the nail with a hammer."
Father: "That's fine."
Bill: "No. It was my thumb nail."

Doctor: "How do you feel today?"
Girl: "With my hands, sir."

Lady: "Are you sleepy?"
Girl: "No. I'm Susan."

Said Father Goat to his son:
    "Stop butting in when I'm talking."

Said the boy to the match:
    "I'm going to strike you."

Said the little stream to the river:
    "You and your big mouth!"

Said Mother Moth to her children:
    "Eat your good wool dinner."

Teacher: "Where is milk stored?"
Girl: "In a cow."

Teacher: "Use the word BARREL
in a sentence."
Jane: "Run or the BARREL bite you."

Teacher: "Johnny, use the word TACKLE in
a sentence."
Johnny: "Anybody who sits on a TACKLE
be sorry."

Pam: "Mother, the dog won't eat the candy I gave him."

Mother: "Well, get rid of the candy."

Pam: "I did. I gave it to Tommy."

Joe: "When do dogs have 12 legs?"

Sam: "I don't know. When do they have 12 legs?"

Joe: "When there are 3 of them."

Boy: "I want a winter coat."
Clerk: "How long?"
Boy: "For the whole winter."

Lady: "Don't cry like that, little girl."
Girl: "Then how shall I cry?"

Jim: "I was on TV today."

Pat: "What fun! How long were you on?"

Jim: "Not very long. As soon as my mother saw me sitting there, she made me get off."

Kathy: "How did you get that bump on your head?"

Tom: "Diving."

Kathy: "Where were you diving?"

Tom: "In the bathtub."

Teacher: "What is the matter, Johnny?"
Johnny: "I itch."
Teacher: "What is making you itch?"
Johnny: "I went to a circus."
Teacher: "Now, Johnny, why would going to a circus make you itch?"
Johnny: "It was a flea circus."

Jill: "Can you spell 'House' with 2 letters?"

Mary: "No. How do you spell 'House' with 2 letters?"

Jill: "TP (teepee)."

Baby Broom was cross and tired. Mother
Broom held Baby Broom close and sang, "Go
to Sweep, Baby. Go to Sweep."